Sum of

When: The Scientific Secrets of Perfect Timing
Daniel H. Pink

Conversation Starters

By BookHabits

Please Note: This is an unofficial conversation starters guide. If you have not yet read the original work or would like to read it again, get the book here.

Copyright © 2017 by BookHabits. All Rights Reserved.
First Published in the United States of America 2017

We hope you enjoy this complementary guide from BookHabits.

Our mission is to aid readers and reading groups with quality, thought provoking material to in the discovery and discussions on some of today's favorite books.

Disclaimer / Terms of Use: Product names, logos, brands, and other trademarks featured or referred to within this publication are the property of their respective trademark holders and are not affiliated with BookHabits. The publisher and author make no representations or warranties with respect to the accuracy or completeness of these contents and disclaim all warranties such as warranties of fitness for a particular purpose. This guide is unofficial and unauthorized. It is not authorized, approved, licensed, or endorsed by the original book's author or publisher and any of their licensees or affiliates.

No part of this publication may be reproduced or retransmitted, electronic or mechanical, without the written permission of the publisher.

Tips for Using BookHabits Conversation Starters:

EVERY GOOD BOOK CONTAINS A WORLD FAR DEEPER THAN the surface of its pages. The characters and their world come alive through the words on the pages, yet the characters and its world still live on. Questions herein are designed to bring us beneath the surface of the page and invite us into the world that lives on. These questions can be used to:

- Foster a deeper understanding of the book
- Promote an atmosphere of discussion for groups
- Assist in the study of the book, either individually or corporately
- Explore unseen realms of the book as never seen before

About Us:

THROUGH YEARS OF EXPERIENCE AND FIELD EXPERTISE, from newspaper featured book clubs to local library chapters, *BookHabits* can bring your book discussion to life. Host your book party as we discuss some of today's most widely read books.

Table of Contents

Introducing *When: The Scientific Secrets of Perfect Timing* 6
Discussion Questions 13
Introducing the Author 34
Fireside Questions 39
Quiz Questions 50
Quiz Answers 63
Ways to Continue Your Reading 64

Introducing *When: The Scientific Secrets of Perfect Timing*

TIME IS ELUSIVE, YET IT IS SOMETHING THAT each one of us has in equal amounts; how is it then, that some seem to garner better results with their time than others? Bestselling author Daniel H. Pink attempts to answer this question in his newest book, "When: The Scientific Secrets of Perfect Timing." While the book's genre is classified as self-help, Pink considers it more of a "when-to" rather than a how-to book. Backed by scientific research findings, the book divulges the hidden secrets of how time affects our mood, motivation, and behavior. Following each chapter, Pink includes a "Time Hacker's Handbook," which includes tips and suggestions for applying this newfound information to our daily routines.

Pink begins with a brief introduction to the "history of time," and reminds readers that time is essentially a human construct; seconds, minutes, and hours only mean what they do to us because of the definitions we have applied to them. Though time is a concept of the human mind, it is a concept that results from the movement of the earth, which gives us a period of daylight and a period of darkness. Time itself might be overlooked as it zips by us without halt, but it is arguably one of the most powerful influences on the human experience. In fact, Pink notes that scientists have been studying the effect of time on the human brain for over one hundred years. Referencing the results of such scientific studies, Pink explains how this information can be applied to nearly every aspect of our daily lives.

As the sun appears to rise and set with each day, our biological clocks follow a consistent daily pattern. Pink cites a research study performed by Michael Macy and Scott Golder that compared tweets from different times of day to "measure people's emotions." What they found, Pink explains, is that people are generally happier in the mornings, experience a downward mood swing in the afternoon, and perk back up again in the evening. What's more is that this pattern of high-low-high showed consistency across the gender, race, religion, and geographic spectrums. Pink explains that each one of us fit into one of three basic chronotypes: Larks (the early birds), Owls (those who naturally thrive in evenings), and Third Birds (the rest of us). Our biological clocks, or "circadian rhythm," may not be entirely in sync with each other's, but the basic pattern remains the same.

The effect of time on our daily lives is further explored with the help of studies that confirm this high-low-high pattern of our biological clocks. For example, Pink refers to a study on the success rate of business calls at differing times of day, which shows more success with morning calls than those placed in the afternoon. Likewise, it appears that more surgical slip-ups occur during afternoon hours than in the morning, and students generally do better with math classes held in the morning versus those held in the afternoon. Pink explains that our minds are sharper in the morning and more capable of thwarting off distractions than they are in the afternoon. In fact, Pink labels this mid-day slump the "Bermuda Triangles of our days."

Understanding the pattern of our biological clocks and how it affects our moods and behavior can help us better plan and manage our time. Pink acknowledges that we don't always have complete control of our daily schedules and offers tips for navigating through the afternoon slumps. For instance, a study in Denmark revealed that students scored higher on tests administered in the morning compared to those who took the same test in the afternoon. However, when afternoon tests followed a break, such as recess, the students' scores were comparable to the morning results. So, while afternoons may pose a challenge for most of us, there are things we can do to turn the least productive part of the day into time well spent.

From scheduling important meetings, appointments, and calls to planning vacations, surgeries, and special events, we're always deciding when to do this or when to do that. Every day we choose how to spend our time, and for many, it seems as if it's always slipping away. However, the key to successful time management may be found in the "hidden science of timing." Daniel H. Pink's "When: The Scientific Secrets of Perfect Timing" offers tips for harnessing the power of time in our own lives by referencing fascinating research studies that emphasize just how important timing is to the human experience.

Discussion Questions

"Get Ready to Enter a New World"

Tip: Begin with questions dealing with broader issues to ensure ample time for quality discussions. Read through all discussion questions before engaging.

~~~

question 1

We each have the same amount of time each day. Why do you think some people make better use of their time than others?

~~~

~~~

question 2

"When: The Scientific Secrets of Perfect Timing" explains that we experience a high-low-high pattern in our days. Why do you think this is?

~~~

~~~

question 3

Do you think that time management is a skill that can be learned or is it a natural trait that some have and some don't? Why so?

~~~

~~~

question 4

"When: The Scientific Secrets of Perfect Timing" explains that afternoons typically coincide with a downward mood swing. Do you find afternoons to be challenging for you? If so, what do you do to overcome this slump?

~~~

~~~

question 5

"When: The Scientific Secrets of Perfect Timing" references studies to support the three chronotypes (Larks, Owls, and Third Birds). Which type are you? How does your chronotype affect your day-to-day life?

~~~

~~~

question 6

How helpful do you find Pink's the "Time Hacker's Handbook" tips? Are there any specific tips you plan to implement?

~~~

~~~

question 7

"When: The Scientific Secrets of Perfect Timing" notes that more surgical slip-ups occur in the afternoon than the morning. What are your feelings about this fact? Do you think the medical field should/could do anything to counteract this?

~~~

~~~

question 8

The book references a study showing that students perform better in morning math classes compared to afternoon math classes. Should all math classes be taught in the morning? Are there any other things that could be done to help students taking afternoon math classes?

~~~

~~~

question 9

"When: The Scientific Secrets of Perfect Timing" explains that our minds are generally more alert in the morning hours than in the afternoon. Do you find yourself more alert in the mornings and more able to ward off distractions? If so, why do you think this is?

~~~

~~~

question 10

Should schools take into consideration the effect of time on our mind and responses? If so, how might things change in the typical school setting?

~~~

~~~

question 11

The book explains that time is a human construct – we defined it. Why do you think we did so?

~~~

~~~

question 12

"When: The Scientific Secrets of Perfect Timing" cites a study in which students performed better on afternoon tests if they were given a break prior to testing. Why do you think that is?

~~~

~~~

question 13

The book opens with a study on Twitter postings that reveals a high-low-high pattern across gender, race, religious, and geographic spectrums. Do you think this pattern is the same for cultures without access to Twitter? Why or why not?

~~~

~~~

question 14

The author notes that scientist have been studying the effect of time on the human brain for over one hundred years. Do you think this is a worthwhile subject to study? Why or why not? What gains do you think we can make from this area of study?

~~~

~~~

question 15

"When: The Scientific Secrets of Perfect Timing" explains that a person's biological clock follows a pattern in which they perk up in the evening. Why do you think this is? Do you experience a pep in the evening as well?

~~~

~~~

question 16

The Wall Street Journal remarked that this book is full of "insight and practical advice." Do you agree with this statement? Why or why not? What did you find most insightful? What advice has helped you the most?

~~~

~~~

question 17

This book is classified as a self-help book, but it is applauded as a "readable narrative" by Penguin Random House. Would you agree with this praise? How is this book different from others you've read on the same subject?

~~~

~~~

question 18

Fans have praised "When: The Scientific Secrets of Perfect Timing." Why do you think this book has been so well-received?

~~~

~~~

question 19

Harper's Bazaar encouraged people to read this book because it "is time well spent." Would you agree with this claim? Why or why not?

~~~

~~~

question 20

Daniel H. Pink has won awards for his previous books. Do you think "When: The Scientific Secrets of Perfect Timing" will/should win any awards? Why or why not?

~~~

Introducing the Author

DANIEL H. PINK WAS BORN ON THE EAST COAST in 1964 but grew up in a small town in Ohio where he graduated high school in 1982. He then attended Northwestern University, where he completed his Bachelor of Arts and graduated with honors. He continued his education at Yale Law School, and though he received his Juris Doctorate, he did not go on to practice law. For a time, Pink worked in politics and previously held the position of chief speechwriter for Vice President Al Gore.

Pink, a bestselling author of nonfiction, tends to write about business, management, technology, and behavioral science. He is a noteworthy journalist, contributing editor, and author, whose articles appear in Wired, The New York Times, and The New Republic. He has published six books, one of which is the first American Manga business book (Manga is a form of Japanese comics). He has been awarded several honorary degrees, and his book "To Sell is Human: The Surprising Truth About Moving Others" was awarded the American Marketing Association's Berry Book Prize. Among his many achievements, Pink also hosted and co-produced the show "Crowd Control," which aired on the National Geographic Channel.

Daniel H. Pink's books have been well-received and have sold over 2 million copies in total. His first book, Washington Post Bestseller "Free Agent Nation: The Future of Working for Yourself" was published in 2001 and was followed by his 2006 New York Times and Business Week bestseller, "A Whole New Mind: Why Right-Brainers Will Rule the Future." Shortly thereafter, Pink published his knock-out career guide, "Johnny Bunko: The Last Career Guide You'll Ever Need." This 2008 publication was the first American business book in Manga format, which is a style of Japanese comics. In 2011, Pink released his New York Times bestseller "Drive: The Surprising Truth About What Motivates Us." Prior to writing "When: The Scientific Secrets of Perfect Timing," Pink published his 2012 book, "To Sell is Human: The Surprising

Truth About Moving Others," which became a #1 Best Seller for New York Times Business, Wall Street Journal Business, and Washington Post.

In addition to his successful writing career, Pink's 2009 TED Talk, "The Puzzle of Motivation," is listed as one of the top ten most viewed TED Talks and has over 19 million views. When asked in an interview for The New Yorker what his writing rules are, he said his number one rule is just to do it, "even when you don't feel like it." Pink has been called an "expert" in the field of "motivation and management" by The Observer, and Publisher's Weekly says reading his work is like finding "your favorite professor in a box."

Daniel H. Pink has published many insightful books and articles. He is a successful speaker and has even hosted a National Geographic television series. Pink writing topics include behavioral science issues, management, and business. Currently, he lives in Washington, D.C. with his wife, Jessica. Together they have three children, two of whom are in college, and one still in high school.

Fireside Questions

"What would you do?"

Tip: These questions can be a fun exercise as it spurs creativity among the readers by allowing alternate scene endings and "if this was you" questions.

~~~

question 21

Daniel H. Pink attended Yale Law School but never practiced law, though he did work for a time in politics. How do you think this has influenced his writing? Or has it?

~~~

~~~

question 22

Do you agree with Daniel H. Pink's number one writing rule: just do it, even when you're feeling unmotivated? Do you think this rule can be applied to other tasks or jobs?

~~~

~~~

question 23

Daniel H. Pink's books have enjoyed great success. Why do you think they have been so well-received? Do you think their success is due to subject matter, writing style, both, or something else?

~~~

~~~

question 24

Daniel H. Pink has been called an "expert" in the field of "motivation and management." Do you agree? By what means do you think he became an expert in these areas?

~~~

~~~

question 25

Daniel H. Pink has written about and given speeches on the topic of motivation. Do you think his newest book, "When: The Scientific Secrets of Perfect Timing" relates to motivation? Why or why not?

~~~

~~~

question 26

Some say that time moves faster now than it did in the past. Do you agree? Based on what you've read in "When: The Scientific Secrets of Perfect Timing," what would you say to someone who believes that time moves faster now than it did previously?

~~~

~~~

question 27

Pink's TED Talk on motivation has over 19 million views. If you were Daniel H. Pink, would you consider presenting a talk on the science of timing? Why or why not?

~~~

~~~

question 28

If you were writing "When: The Scientific Secrets of Perfect Timing" would you cover any addition topics that Daniel H. Pink did not address? If so, what topics?

~~~

~~~

question 29

Daniel H. Pink reminds us that time is a human concept. Though we have created the concept of time, do you think we can un-create it? Could we ever live in a world without the concept of time? If so, how would things be different?

~~~

~~~

question 30

Pink's 2008 publication, "The Adventures of Johnny Bunk: The Last Career Guide You'll Ever Need" is written in Manga (Japanese Comic) format. Do you think "When: The Scientific Secrets of Perfect Timing" could have been written in Manga as well? Would the message be different? If so, how?

~~~

Quiz Questions

"Ready to Announce the Winners?"

Tip: Create a leaderboard and track scores to see who gets the most correct answers. Winners required. Prizes optional.

quiz question 1

The author calls "When: The Scientific Secrets of Perfect Timing" a _____ book rather than a how-to book.

~~~

quiz question 2

Pink notes in the book that time is a concept of the human _____.

~~~

~~~

quiz question 3

The general pattern of our biological clocks is
_____-_____-_____.

~~~

~~~

quiz question 4

The three chronotypes are: _____

___.

~~~

~~~

quiz question 5

True or False: Pink calls afternoons the "Bermuda Triangles" of our day.

~~~

~~~

quiz question 6

True or False: The Twitter study referenced in the book found that people were happier in the mornings and afternoons than they were in the evenings.

~~~

~~~

quiz question 7

True or False: Science has only been studying the effect of time on the human mind and experience for the past fifty years.

~~~

~~~

quiz question 8

Daniel H. Pink has published a total of _____ books.

~~~

~ ~ ~

quiz question 9

Daniel H. Pink has been called an expert in the fields of _____ and _____.

~ ~ ~

~~~

quiz question 10

Pink's knock-out career guide was written in _____ form.

~~~

~~~

quiz question 11

True or False: Daniel H. Pink gave a successful TED Talk on motivation.

~~~

~~~

quiz question 12

True or False: Daniel H. Pink graduated from Yale Law School and practiced law for three years before focusing on his writing career.

~~~

Quiz Answers

1. When-to
2. Mind
3. High-Low-High
4. Larks, Owls, and Third Birds
5. True
6. False; the Twitter study found that people were happier in the mornings and evenings.
7. False; science has been studying the effect of time for over 100 years
8. Six
9. Motivation and management
10. Manga
11. True
12. False; though Pink graduated from Yale Law School, he has never practiced law

Ways to Continue Your Reading

EVERY month, our team runs through a wide selection of books to pick the best titles for readers and reading groups, and promotes these titles to our thousands of readers – sometimes with free downloads, sale dates, and additional brochures.

If you have not yet read the original work or would like to read it again, get the book here.

Want to register yourself or a book group? It's free and takes 1-click.

Register here.

On the Next Page…

Please write us your reviews! Any length would be fine but we'd appreciate hearing you more! We'd be SO grateful.

Till next time,

BookHabits

"Loving Books is Actually a Habit"

CPSIA information can be obtained
at www.ICGtesting.com
Printed in the USA
LVHW090503050719
623252LV00001B/26/P